THE MARK OF CAIN

ISIAH BAITY JR

ARPress
ILLUMINATING IDEAS,
EMPOWERING VOICES

ARPress
45 Dan Road Suite 5
Canton MA 02021
Hotline: 1(888) 821-0229
Fax: 1(508) 545-7580

Ordering Information:
Quantity sales. Special discounts are available on quantity purchases by corporations, associations, and others. For details, contact the publisher at the address above.

Printed in the United States of America.

ISBN-13:   Paperback   979-8-89676-179-2
           eBook   979-8-89676-180-8

Library of Congress Control Number: 2025913071

CONTENTS

PREFACE

I feel honor and extreme gratitude to my readers for allowing me to inspire them with my two books, *The Power of Love (Luv)* and *The Power of Love (Luv II), The Other Side.* However, *The Mark of Cain* has been the most compelling for me to write. I would always put off writing it. I would come up with various excuses why I should not write it, but the Mark of Cain was always right there staring me in the face. (It is a book of truth and facts.) I wonder how many people experience this, but will never speak out. Indeed, how many of you are experiencing it right now, but bury it in the depths of your heart and ignore it? After reading *The Mark of Cain*, many readers will be able to identify with this experience and validate this book. Now that the book is finished, I can finally breathe a sigh of relief, because I feel that writing it was one of my main missions in life.

ONE

THE EARLY YEARS

One evening long ago I was watching television and heard a Klansman spouting his views about the Mark of Cain. His explanation would trouble and baffle me for the next twenty years. That mark was in such great contrast to my life and people like me, that it constantly raised the question in my heart, "Could this be true? Could this Klansman be right?" Immediately after hearing the Klansman's view, I decided to study my life and see if it paralleled the Mark of Cain. First, we must examine this mark, when it came about, as well as where, and why it came about, and who initially received the mark.

In the Bible, the fourth chapter of Genesis talks about Adam and Eve having two sons, Cain and Abel. The day came when both sons presented themselves before the altar to offer sacrifices to God. Now Abel was a cheerful, generous giver and God accepted his love offering. Cain was stingy and his heart was not right, and God would not accept Cain's offering. Cain became jealous, found his brother Abel in the field, and killed him. And God said, "What hast thou done,

Cain? The voice of thy brother's blood crieth unto me from the ground." God cursed Cain and made him a fugitive and vagabond on the earth. And the Lord set a Mark upon Cain.

Now that we have identified this mark, let us look at some events in my life, and others like me, and see how the Klansman's beliefs at first seemed to be so profoundly true. The first sign that I may have bore the Mark was in 1960, Xn I was five years old. My father and mother had taken me to a department store. I became thirsty for water. The water fountains were in the area where Mom and Dad were shopping. I went to this sparkling clean water fountain and began to drink.

My parents were not aware of what I was doing, but when a white policeman yelled, "Boy, get out of that water fountain!" it caught their attention.

My dad rushed to me and grabbed me from the fountain. He looked into the eyes of the angry, stone-faced policeman and humbly apologized for my actions. I couldn't understand what was going on. Dad then looked at me and began to explain.

"You see this water fountain that you were drinking from. It's not allowed. Never do that again. This fountain is for white folks only. Always check the fountain to see whether it says 'White' or 'Colored.' See here, son, this fountain reads, 'White.' The whole family could be in big trouble just because of this."

Then I asked, "But where can I drink, Daddy?"

He took me about twenty feet down the hall to another water fountain; over it was the word "Colored."

"This is our fountain, son" Daddy said.

As I gazed at this fountain, my thirst went away. It was dirty, nasty, and smelly. It looked like it hadn't been cleaned in months.

No thanks, Dad. I'll wait till I get home," I said.

The restroom was behind the water fountain. Dad pointed to it.

"See this restroom, son? It's the same as with the fountain. This restroom is 'Colored'-it's the one you use. Never go in the one that says 'White.'"

Dad needed to relieve himself, so he took me into this 'Colored' restroom. When I entered, my stomach churned, I almost vomited because of the smell and filth. I asked Daddy if I could wait outside, because I was about to puke. When I went outside, I made up my mind that no matter what, I would never drink from that Colored fountain or use that Colored restroom. I would just simply wait until I got back home.

I did not associate this incident with the Mark because I was only five and knew nothing of it. However, it was then that I first realized that something wasn't right and that I was different. Somehow, I knew that this incident would later resurface and become a positive factor in my life, in contrast to what the Klansman had said about the Mark of Cain.

Later that same year, a similar event occurred. A carnival was in town. Every day my parents and I walked by it on our way into town, and each time I would start shouting.

"Mama, Daddy, stop! I want to ride the ponies." I cried so much one day that my dad stopped.

"Come on, son, let's ride the pony," said Dad. I was so happy that my wish had come true. My dad was a humble, friendly man, and he now approached the carnival man.

"How do you do, sir?" Dad asked with a smile.

"What can I do for you?" the carnival man asked.

While Dad and the carnival man talked, I watched the other kids having so much fun riding the ponies. I couldn't wait until it was my turn. I had already picked out the pony I wanted to ride. Then it came, the most devastating event in my childhood.

"How much for my son to ride a pony?" my dad asked.

The carnival man looked Dad in the eyes.

"We don't let niggers ride," he said.

"Okay," Dad said. "Let's go, son." He took my hand, and we headed toward the exit. I couldn't understand. My wish was shattered so quickly-by a few words. I was deeply hurt.

The tears rolled down my face.

"What's a nigger?" I asked Daddy. That was the first time I had ever heard that word.

"A nigger is a bad word that some bad people use for colored people. You are not a nigger. You are a colored boy. Forget what that carnival man said and forget about his ponies. They're not worth riding," my dad told me.

I could not understand why I was hated so much for nothing. This would also rise up in my life again and make the Mark of Cain a valid argument.

A few years passed, and it had become increasingly evident to me that I was different and didn't have the same privileges as others. Even though I couldn't understand it, I simply accepted it. In the 1960s, when I was about eleven years old, I experienced a turning point in my life. I happened to be watching the news. I saw a preacher who looked like me. It was Martin L. King, Jr., saying things, like "we are all created equal" and "man should not be judged by the color of his skin." My favorite quote of his was, "One day we will all join hands and live together in harmony." These words sounded sweet to my ears, but I didn't think it was possible because of the great opposition of white people who didn't want change.

As I continued to follow Dr. King through the news and witness the beatings, hangings, bombings, and police dogs tearing at the colored human flesh, my hopes for the dream slowly died. These horrible images stayed in my memory, and later came to mind concerning the Mark of Cain. In 1970, as I entered high school, many things were changing. Busing had just started, and my father had become a minister, but to me, things had not changed very much for my race. My mother and father always taught us to love everybody, but in a black history course, these lessons seemed more fantasy than reality. In class, we watched films of despicable things that whites had done to us. The books we read were just as horrible. Our teacher expounded on these events in such a way that when class was over, we were all in a rage. This volcano of anger finally erupted into one of the worst riots in the state of Florida. Many high school students, black and white, male and female, were badly wounded, yet absolutely nothing was accomplished by this riot.

When the dust settled and the school was somewhat back to normal, the hatred for both races continued to simmer under the surface. Blacks kept to themselves, and so did whites. When they did meet in the halls, classrooms, or outside the building, both races taunted each other with words of hate.

Meanwhile, I decided to change my major from electrical wiring to agriculture. I don't know why-I certainly did not like agriculture. I guess I just didn't care anymore. It seemed like I was born to be damned no matter what I might do. I just wanted an easy way to get my diploma and get out of high school. My transfer was granted, but little did I know that I was in for a big surprise.

On the first day of class, I can remember knocking on the agriculture class door. The teacher came to the door, inspected my transfer papers and invited me in. When I stepped into that class, I think my heart stopped. I felt like a small fly in a sea of milk. The whole agriculture class was white. These were the same guys we had rioted against. What made it worse was that the leader of the Klan, Big Bo, was also in the class. I knew I had walked into the lion's den.

"Class, we have a new student, Isaiah Baity," the teacher announced. The boys snickered and joked, with Big Bo initiating the whole ordeal. I focused my eyes on him, with his big cowboy hat and an unlit cigar in his mouth and a huge Confederate flag on the back of his jacket. I wanted to punch him just as bad as he did me.

The teacher had to step out of class for something, and Bo didn't waste any time making me aware of his presence. He sent his flunky, Red Richie, over to feel me out and relay his messages. Red smiled and acted friendly, but I knew what was behind his actions. Most of Red's conversation was about Bo, but I already knew about him. I knew he was the captain of the wrestling team and had never been beaten and that he intimidated many people. Nonetheless, I was confident in myself; I was a star football player, in great shape, and not afraid of Bo. Red ended his welcome-to-class conversation with a warning.

"Watch your back. Bo doesn't like you," he said.

"I don't like him either. Tell him that he'd better watch his back," was my reply.

As the days passed, I could feel the tension and hatred growing between Bo and me. In the midst of our confrontation, there was something else brewing that Bo didn't know about. I knew because I had overheard a conversation. Danny, another redneck racist, envied Bo. Danny felt he should be the leader of the whites. He had persuaded some of the guys to follow him. He was going to catch Bo off guard and beat him to a pulp. He figured the whole class would see the beating and spread it throughout the school, making Danny the new leader. Because Danny's desk was close to mine, I overheard these plans.

The next day I was sitting in class. The teacher had not yet arrived, when Bo came strutting in with his trademark cowboy hat and the cigar in his mouth. Danny's desk was next to the back door where Bo had come in. Danny jumped Bo from behind and landed vicious blows to Bo's head. The cowboy hat flew off his head, and the cigar flew across the room. Big Bo went down between the desks. Danny pulled a large hook knife from his jacket and drew it back to strike a likely fatal blow. In that moment, I believe Mom and Dad's teaching came back to me. I no longer saw Bo as a racist bigot, but rather as an ignorant, helpless idiot, who had been sucker-punched, and was about to lose his life. I jumped from my desk and grabbed Danny's arm, preventing the hook knife from coming down on Bo. I slammed Danny on top of the desk and banged the hand with the knife. Red Richie and a couple more guys rushed over and pried the knife from Danny's hand.

Bo had been saved by his worst enemy. Moreover, it was probably the first time a man of my color had ever done anything for him. He looked at me with surprise and gratitude. While Red and the other guys restrained Danny, I stretched out my hand to Bo. He took hold, and I lifted him from the floor.

"Thanks, man," he said.

Those were the first words he had ever spoken to me, and they were the beginning of a genuine and unlikely friendship that would last forever. Danny was suspended, and Bo and I got to know each other better and became closer and closer. Two weeks later, after Bo felt more comfortable with me, he disclosed that the day Danny attacked him was the day he and his boys were planning to attack me.

"I'm glad things happened this way, because I found a true friend," he said. "I called off the attack on you and I let it be known that anybody who attacks you is going to have to face me."

That was good, but I had concentrated on Bo so much, I had neglected my own race. Among the blacks, we had no single leader, but there were several whose words carried a lot of weight, and I was one of them. The black students met in the long hallway smoking area. Whites would not go in this area because they knew it was off limits.

After breaking away from Bo, I went to the smoking area to meet with my black brothers. Word had gotten back to them that I had been hanging around the most hideous and hated white on campus. I held my peace while they accused and threatened me. Although I was strong among my people, I also knew that they hated Bo so much that if I said the wrong thing, they would attack me. The discussion that day was about Bo daring to walk through the smoking area, especially, with that big Confederate flag on his back. I knew nothing of this. The decision was made that the next time Bo did this, he would be stomped down to a pulp.

After leaving the smoking area, I immediately went to see Bo. I tried to convince him to stay out of the smoking area and to stop wearing the jacket with the Confederate flag on campus. Bo was bull-headed and wouldn't listen. He just looked at me with that devious smile and that cigar in his mouth and nodded his head.

"I just love a challenge," was all he would say.

"Bo," I said, "if you are really my friend, you won't do this crazy thing, man, because you are going down, and I'll be going down along with you. What are you trying to prove, Bo?" He would not listen to me. At this point, I felt like Bo had a serious problem or a death wish. I knew I had to do something or this fool was going to get himself killed.

When I went to school the next day, I went to the smoking area early to talk to my brothers. While the brothers shot the breeze, talking about the fine ladies, I decided to change the subject.

"Fellows, you know that redneck Bo? He's crazy, but he saved my ass the other day. I was outnumbered fifty-to-one, and those whites were going to rumble on me, but Bo stopped them. I don't think he's all that bad, but just crazy as hell. If he comes through here with that flag on, let's just ignore him. I'm sure it'll hurt him more than an ass whipping, because he's only doing it for attention."

The brothers listened, but I didn't know whether they had heard me or not. I hoped they did because as soon as I looked up, Bo was walking down the smoking hall. He had his cowboy hat on, the cigar in his mouth, and that Confederate flag on his jacket. All the nerves in my body tensed up. All I was thinking and feeling in my heart was, "that stupid fool." As he walked by, something astonishing happened. All the brothers began turning their backs to Bo as though he wasn't there. I knew they must have heard me.

"Thank you, Jesus," I said to myself softly. Bo passed through safely because brothers decided to do it my way.

Later, I saw Bo.

"You know, you did a stupid thing this morning," I told him.

"Nothing was going to happen to me," he said. "Those niggers are afraid of me."

"Niggers? Niggers!" I said. "Who in the hell are you calling niggers? If you're calling them niggers, you're calling me one. We are the same. We might as well end this friendship, and we can get down right now because I am not afraid of you."

Bo called me by my nickname.

"Ike, if you're not niggers, what are you? I grew up in the country away from everyone. I rarely saw people like you and your brothers, and when I did, my father would say, 'That's a damn nigger. They are lazy, good-for-nothing carpetbaggars. Never trust a nigger, son, and never have one as a friend.' This is what I was taught. Nigger was the common word to identify people like you."

Then I remembered the riots. There was an instance with this white kid who was about fifteen years old. He had been caught up in a large swarm of blacks. The black dude that got to him first, punched him in the face, and the kid fell down. The black dude got on top of him and lifted him by the collar of his shirt, and said, "Who am I?"

All the white kid could say in a trembling voice was, "A nigger."

"Who am I?" the black guy shouted while he shook him by the collar.

The kid's voice had become weaker, but he still said, "A nigger."

The black guy pounded him in the face. This went on until the white boy's face was a bloody mess. Every time he was asked, the white kid's answer to the black guy was always, "nigger." It didn't end until he couldn't speak anymore. I felt sorry for the kid, but each time he said the word nigger, my sorrow lessened. I later found out that the white kid didn't know any better. It was the way he was raised, just like Bo.

Bo's ignorance rekindled my anger. I explained to him that it would take some time, but he had to break out of his bad habits.

"Never use that word nigger to a black person, even the word colored isn't acceptable anymore, especially among the blacks my age and younger. Always refer to us as 'blacks.' If a black person calls his own a nigger, we're usually not affected by it, but if you or another white person said this to us, we would be offended. My generation of blacks will not be like our fathers. With them, the word nigger was used freely. The new generation of blacks will rise up in opposition when you use this word, and even your life could be in danger. Bo, you must change your way of thinking about blacks, and your vocabulary. You can no longer isolate yourself from us. The times are changing, and we all have to live together. It would be better to get along."

I didn't address the remarks about the brothers being afraid of Bo. If I did, I was sure he would have tried that stunt in the smoking area again, and the next time he might not be so lucky.

It would be years before I revealed to him that it was my words that they listened to and saved him in the smoking area that day. I think I actually got through to Bo, because day-by-day, week-by-week, and month-by-month I noticed a significant change in him. Sometimes when he would forget and almost say the N-word, he would catch himself, and say, "I mean black."

In the months to come, Bo and I would spend a lot of time together. I believed that I had grown on him, and through me, he could see that not all black people were lazy or good-for-nothings and that we loved and had feelings just like any other race. He began to see how he might have missed the pleasure of having a good friend, only because of the color he saw. Bo and I graduated from high school. Bo got a high-paying job in a chemical plant, and I went off to a black college in Mississippi. It would not be the end of our friendship. We remain close, even today.

Two

Learning Experience

The first day I arrived at college in Mississippi, another instance occurred that caused me to look at myself, and ask myself "Why?" After the first day of orientation, I settled into my dormitory. I made new friends with other freshmen like me, and we all had one thing in common; we were all black. We decided to tour the campus, and after our campus stroll was complete, six of us ventured into the city. It was not long before our sightseeing was disrupted by a vanload of white guys. They came by, yelling at us.

"Get the hell back where you belong, niggers!"

Then they took grapefruits that they had in the van and began to throw them at us with great force. Two of my friends were hit square in the face. As I turned to run, they nailed me in the back. The pain was awesome from that lick, but I kept on running. We all scattered and ran. We didn't know where we were going but we kept on running. When I figured those guys were no longer chasing us, I stopped running and tried to figure out where I was. After walking for some time and asking directions to get back to the dormitory, I finally made it back. My five friends were already there, but I almost didn't recognize them. Faces were swollen, lips were busted, and eyes were bruised. They were not the only victims. My back had a welt left by a grapefruit, and it hurt every time I moved. As I gazed upon my friends and felt the pain in my back, I said in my heart, "Oh, God, why do you allow things like this to happen?" My heart ached, while tears ran down my cheeks. "Why, Lord?" I asked. "You made us. We didn't make ourselves. I am sure, the way things are down here, if we had a choice in the matter, I doubt there would be one black person. Lord, help me understand."

A month passed, but the grapefruit incident was still fresh in my mind. One night I got a call from my mother. She said my father had taken ill and she wanted me to come home. I explained the situation to my teachers and caught a bus home. My family was happy to see me, but Dad was in the hospital with unknown seizures and pain in his head. After about a week, Dad began to get better. It was good news that Dad was going to be all right and I would be returning to college soon.

One day while I was home, I was watching a talk show, and this Klansman got up and said something that would alter my life. This was my introduction to the Mark of Cain that I have previously mentioned. I hated everything he said, but I couldn't ignore the truth. To me, what he said was truth because I was living it. During the program, the Klansman took a piece of Scripture from the Bible and explained his theory.

"In Genesis, the eleventh through the sixteenth verses

of the fourth chapter tell us that Cain was a stingy, jealous murderer, just like niggers. God said that Cain would be a fugitive over all the earth," he said to the audience. My blood began to boil.

"Isn't that what niggers are?" he asked, looking for support from the people in the studio and the host. "If you whites would admit it, you would know it's true. For instance, if you invite a nigger into your home, you keep a close eye on him because he steals. It's his nature because God has cursed him. Ladies, if you were on the elevator with one, you would cling tightly to your purse because he robs." The Klansman had a list of examples ready to go for the hooting and hollering audience.

"On television, who do you usually see caught by surveillance cameras while they rob convenience stores, run through shopping malls with stolen goods, and steal cars? It's the damn niggers. It's the curse. God also said that Cain would be a vagabond throughout the earth. Look at the niggers. Just like Cain, they are aimless wanderers. They wander through life, stealing, robbing, and cheating. They have no purpose. Sometimes an 'uppity' nigger gets a little money and feels important and thinks he can fit in with the whites. They are only fooling themselves because no amount of money can remove the Mark of Cain. They are just drifters, cast out by God.

"God said even the earth wouldn't yield her strength to Cain, nor will it yield to niggers. Haven't you noticed, no matter how hard some niggers work, they never have anything. God lets them go so far and then cuts them off. The nigger is in debt for his entire life. When he buys a brand new car, he wants society to think that he is doing well, like the white man, but follow him home and see where he lives. I guarantee it's a shack with a bunch of little niggers and a pregnant wife that he don't take care of." The Klansman wasn't well spoken, but people were actually buying his message of hate. I couldn't believe it.

"God said Cain would be hidden from his face. A lot of niggers go to church. They pray and carry on, but God's not listening to them, and God doesn't care about them. They are cursed, and God said everyone would know them. God put a mark on Cain, and that mark has been handed down from Cain to the niggers. The Mark of Cain is the curse of being colored."

I was devastated by what the Klansman had said. Not only had he trampled my race, but he had also accused God of initiating my troubles. I thought back to the time of the water fountain and restroom. I thought about Bo and being hit by the grapefruit. All the negative days of my black past flashed before my eyes. I thought if God condoned what the Klansman had said, life would be meaningless to all blacks. Would we be doomed in this world and in the world to come? The God I know is a God of love and a righteous judge. Shouldn't the judge of all the earth do right?

It was hard for me to believe what the Klansman had said about God, but he seemed so convincing. My father was a Baptist minister, and I remembered his sermons and the church teachings about God scattering the people across the earth. That was the explanation of different colors and races that I knew. Now I was not absolutely sure. My negative experiences forced me to believe the Klansman's speech. I hid this secret and my feelings about the Mark of Cain, but I was determined to seek God's voice for answers. I began the second chapter of my life as a black man.

Bo found out I was back in town, and he invited me to a company barbecue. My self-esteem was low, but I wanted to see Bo, so I decided to accept the invitation. There was Bo with all his coworkers, mostly white, when I arrived. He jumped up immediately and hugged me. He introduced me as his best friend. We were very happy to see each other. We talked about old times and new adventures, laughed together, danced with the ladies, and enjoyed the picnic. We just had a good time. It briefly took my mind off the Mark of Cain.

When the barbecue was over, Bo suggested that we go to a restaurant for breakfast. I agreed, but when we pulled into the parking lot of the restaurant, I could see that only whites were in there. I felt threatened and out of place until I saw the police officers through the window. When Bo and I walked in, I felt all eyes on me. It made me uncomfortable. The waitress greeted Bo and he asked for a table for two.

"You can have a table for two, but he (referring to me) can't sit at it," she said to Bo.

"Why?" asked Bo.

"We don't serve coloreds," she said plainly, not even worried that I was standing right there, listening. Bo argued with the waitress about this matter while I looked to the policemen for help. They wouldn't say a word; they just kept on eating. One officer looked at me with a grin on his face, as though he agreed with the waitress that I was not welcome. I touched Bo on the shoulder and told him to go ahead and eat.

"I'm not hungry," I told him, "just tired, and since I drove my own car, I can find my way back home."

Bo yelled at the waitress.

"If he can't eat here, I can't eat here. I'll never come in this damn place again." When Bo and I were leaving the restaurant, he apologized for what had happened. "I'm glad I'm not like those ignorant people anymore, thanks to you." I convinced Bo that I was tired and needed to get home, but the real reason was the Mark of Cain ringing in my ears. Even though he stood up for me, I was feeling uncomfortable, even with Bo.

For the rest of that night and for days to come, I dwelled on what the Klansman had said, and how I had been treated in the restaurant. I saw myself as a fugitive and a vagabond. The idea that I was an unwanted outcast on the earth became more valid. From that time on, I focused my attention on God. I needed to know Him better and develop a sound understanding of the Mark of Cain. I wanted to know how He felt about the blacks He had created. Beginning with the first page, I began to study and examine the Holy Bible slowly and carefully.

After a few weeks, my father's health had returned and he had come home from the hospital. He and my mother would have been proud if they knew I was studying the Bible, but I kept it a secret because I knew they would give me their views about the mark of Cain. I wanted to find the answers for myself and was prepared to accept the truth as reality. When my father's health improved, my mother told me I could go back to school. I could tell she was concerned about my leaving, but she had little idea that my whole mindset had changed. If the Mark of Cain was true, it wouldn't have mattered if I finished school and got a good job. If God had cursed me, I was doomed. I also didn't want to go back because of the experience I had off campus, and being confined to campus would be like prison-boxed in. Venturing off campus was a chance. It wasn't worth living in fear. I told Mom I would take the rest of this year off and find a job to help. I could always go back to school later. My choice turned out to be the right one.

Later that year, my dad had a stroke that left him paralyzed on one side, and my mom fell and broke her arm in three places. Even though our family was close, with three brothers and one sister, I was the only one available to take proper care of them.

I took my first job at a major lumber company. The company brought in day laborers to work during the busy Christmas season. The day laborers were not treated well. The company managers felt that the day laborers were at the bottom of the barrel and all they wanted was a day's pay to buy crack or get drunk. The company didn't mind bringing them in to work, because they worked hard and, most of all, they worked cheap. I was a regular at the lumber company, and I got to know most of the guys there. I found that there is a terrible myth that society has put on the downtrodden and poor.

For example, when I first started work, I believed, like society, that the day laborers just didn't want to work. They just wanted to get enough money to get their groove on and get high. Every Friday, they would jump for joy, while yelling out, "I got some duckies in my pocket. I am going to get me a chicken head tonight." (A chicken head is a woman who will perform any kind of sexual act for the least bit of money to support her crack habit.)

These guys didn't care about the company or each other.

If you got in their way or said something they didn't like, they would become violent and possibly hurt you. I watched these guys for months. They squandered their few pennies for meaningless pleasure and had no goal or hope for the future. When I looked at them, I saw myself. We were hopeless wanderers branded with the Mark of Cain.

Society's myth that these people were total losers came into view when permanent job openings were available. The day laborers were told that they had a chance at these positions. Their whole outlook on life suddenly changed. Their self-esteem improved, the chicken head talks began to diminish, and they became more courteous to coworkers. They finally had hope for a good job and benefits. These guys were working so hard that they made me feel a little leery about my job security. I knew in my heart then that all these guys needed was a chance. They were looked upon as bums and losers for so long, they now believed it.

The opportunities built up their morale and self-esteem and gave them back respect. They were very seldom talking about crack and meaningless ventures, but instead they were talking about what they were going to do for their sons and daughters and how they were going to get off of the street and make a better life for themselves.

One day, the lumber company announced a major layoff and all the hopes and dreams went up in smoke. The day laborers were laid off immediately, and I was part of the lot. I grieved more for the other guys than for myself. I had a safety net. I had my family, but many of them had nobody. I watched their self-esteem drop as the wind was taken out of their sails. They had worked so hard to prove that they could hold a steady job and be productive in society, but now it was back to the streets, sleeping under bridges, and begging for nickels and dimes. I grieved greatly for them and put another check in the column for the Mark of Cain.

Later, I worked as a microfilm technician. I would take Mom and Dad to therapy, pay bills and order groceries. My brothers and sisters would help every chance they had. All of my new responsibilities distracted my thinking and my obsession with the Mark of Cain. I would still study the Bible every chance I got. There were instances, even while I was caring for my mom and dad that kept the Mark of Cain from being completely forgotten. One was when Mom went into the grocery store.

I had decided to stay in the car with Dad. We talked, and I read my Bible. While I sat in the driver's seat reading, Dad was in the back relaxing; since his stroke, he always took the back seat. We were parked right in front of the store. I always used the handicap space, but we had the proper handicap sticker on the tag. I noticed an armored truck pull up. My father was paying more attention to the female guard who got out of the truck than I was.

"Son, look, look!" Dad said to me. I was surprised when I looked up from my reading and was suddenly facing the barrel of a gun. When the security guard saw me, she had unholstered her weapon and pointed at me until she went into the store to pick up the money. Dad couldn't believe what he had just seen. He was shocked. He said with fright, "Son if you had moved, she probably would have shot you." He kept saying it over and over and told me it was a shame and that it wasn't right.

Before I could say anything, the female guard exited the store and repeated the same process as she had on the way in.

Her gun and eyes stayed on me until she got into the truck with the moneybag and left. My dad couldn't believe it. "That's a shame," he kept saying and insisted that her actions be reported.

"To who?" I asked him. "Have I ever been in trouble or been in jail? Do I look like an alien from another planet?" My dad reassured me that I was a good son. I wanted him to tell me why she had pointed that gun at me. Before he could answer though, I told him my own reason: it was because I was black. Dad's idea of telling her boss what she had done would be like telling a brick wall. It would mean nothing to him, even if he believed it. Dad told me it was God who would make things right. All those who had been mistreating us would eventually be punished by God.

The Mark of Cain rose to the forefront of my mind. Would God punish them, or were we the ones being punished? When Mom came out of the store, Dad couldn't wait to tell her what had happened. While they expressed their opinions with anger, I didn't say a word. I was shocked by the incident, but not surprised. I had already been exposed to similar acts of hatred. When Mom finally calmed down, we went to finish our errands. We drove around the corner to the post office to get stamps. When I pulled into the post office parking lot, I parked in a disabled space, just like at the store. It was less than a few minutes before a deputy sheriff pulled behind me and blocked me in. He jumped from his car rushed over to me and asked where our handicap sticker was. Before I could answer, he reached for his pad and pencil.

"I'm tired of you people parking illegally," he said and began to write out a two-hundred-fifty-dollar ticket. I tried to explain calmly that I had a handicap sticker on the car. I tried to point out that my father was sitting in the back and had a cane from a stroke. He didn't care that my mother, who was inside, had a broken arm. The officer still only wanted to know about the sticker.

"It's on the tag," I told him. When the officer saw the sticker on the tag, he became outraged at the employee who worked in the post office who had reported us. The officer, who was white, actually apologized to me. He said that people would never change. They were stuck on stereotypes. The officer went inside the post office and Mom came out. She always missed the action.

Another similar incident occurred shortly after that. My mother had gone into the mall. Once again, my dad and I were waiting in the parking lot. We were parked legally in the handicap parking and, just like before, sheriffs and security swarmed around us. Unlike the deputy at the post office, this one had a violent and angry attitude. He asked for my driver's license and registration. I asked him what I had done, but he wouldn't answer me. While he was running me through the computer, all the flashing lights from the police cars and security caused a big scene. Customers and employees were all looking at me, and I was being looked upon as a major criminal. After the computer check, the officer came back to my car.

"What have I done?" I asked him. Then he began to berate and hassle me about the handicap sticker. While he rambled on, I felt a sinking feeling inside, and even though I had no record, I thought he was going to take me to jail.

After the officer had yelled in my face for a couple of minutes, he waited for an answer about the handicap sticker. I politely explained that when he ran the tag through the computer, he should have seen the handicap sticker. When he looked again and saw that the proper sticker was on the tag, he wouldn't apologize. He had been outdone. He and another officer began to leave, but he yelled a last warning to me.

"If I catch you parked in a handicap space alone, I'll fine you and throw you in jail!"

Even though Dad was much older than I, and had seen many things done to blacks, this would be the last time he would ride with Mom and me for shopping. The harassment had even gotten to him. The mark of Cain was beating down on me. It was becoming more and more evident that the mark was the mark of the black man. One of the most jolting experiences I had concerning the mark of Cain was when I went into a well-known drug store. It was in the wintertime, and I had a regular black jacket on. I smoked a pipe, and I had previously purchased some pipe tobacco. I was going to buy more when I walked into the drugstore. When I walked in, the security scanner went off.

There were two cashiers at the front of the store while the alarm was going off. I kept walking toward the manager and cashiers. Suddenly one cashier screamed out that I had a gun. The other cashier screamed, and the manager looked at me with fright. I told them I didn't have a gun and then pulled the almost empty pack of tobacco out of my jacket. When they finally calmed down, they realized that the security buzzer went off because the security patch hadn't been taken off the pipe tobacco. While they tried to apologize, I couldn't accept it. I told the cashier that if a cop or security officer had heard her yell about a gun, they probably would have shot and killed an unarmed man-all over an almost empty pack of pipe tobacco. I turned and walked away and never returned to that store again.

The pipe tobacco situation made me feel that the Mark of Cain was upon me, and what made it seem more evident occurred shortly after that incident. In the same complex as the drug store, was a well-known grocery store. Billy Ferry, a former schoolmate of mine, walked into that grocery store carrying a gasoline can, and talking to himself. The reason I know the facts is, my brother was in the store and witnessed it. Thank God, my brother got his items and left. What happened next was a major catastrophe. Billy, with his gasoline, set fire to that grocery store, taking many innocent lives and disabling and disfiguring others forever. How could this happen? I asked myself this question repeatedly. Everybody that knew Billy knew that he was a mental case and needed help. But just one door down from the grocery store was that drug store cashier who was terrified of me, not because I was carrying a gasoline can, or a weapon, but because of my black face. My perspective was that because Billy was white, he blended and mixed in with the people and never was confronted about the gasoline can.

I truly felt if it had been me carrying that gas, I would have been confronted immediately, and escorted out of the store. Because of this incident, the Mark of Cain became a reality and a certainty in my life.

Every time I went into a store, I was always followed. Whether it was aisle six or eight, whatever aisle I was on, I would soon hear a call on store's intercom to go to that aisle. I was used to this, but not what happened in the drugstore. Each incident seemed to cut away at my self-esteem, confidence, and outgoing personality. It made me retreat into a shell and withdraw from society. When meeting whites in passing, even if they had a smile on their face, I felt that it was a disguise. When approaching them, I wanted to hide my face because I knew how I was perceived. Being a tall muscular black man, I felt I had to smile and present myself in a friendly manner. I didn't want to be looked upon as a fugitive or make people afraid of me. I just wanted to be seen as a man, but that was impossible. I had two strikes against me: I was big and I was black. Even though I hated how I was accused and perceived, for some reason I couldn't hate the people who saw me that way.

My love remained steadfast for all people. Whenever I was in the company of whites, I would go out of my way to be a humble kind man. I didn't want anything from people except the same that I had given them, respect and love. Even though I had begun to withdraw from society because of the bumps from the Mark of Cain, my hunger and thirst for the knowledge of God intensified.

One day, while I was home with my sister, my hunger and thirst were satisfied. While we were watching television, my heart started to beat irregularly and I had pain in my chest. I didn't mention it to my sister until the pain was so strong, I couldn't stand it anymore. When I told her that I was having chest pain, she rushed me to the emergency room. While lying on a stretcher, hooked up to monitors, with tubes in my nose and needles in my arms, I was in excruciating pain. I thought that this was the end for me. I always believed God was the one that brings the heart to a halt. I thought that all my questioning about the Mark of Cain was not acceptable to Him. Now He would shut my mouth for good.

In that moment, I did something I had never done before.

I began to speak out to Him with sincerity. I told the Lord how I had studied His word, but that I didn't really know Him. I thought that He was ending my life. I had read all about hell, and I was afraid to go there, but I trusted that heaven was a beautiful place to be. I wasn't afraid of dying, because for me, there wasn't much to this world. God has said that if a person believed in His son, He would save him. I did believe, and if that wasn't enough, could He really save *me* or my mother and father.

Suddenly, the hospital room became ten times brighter. The chest pain went away. God spoke to me, not in an audible voice, but He revealed his word to my mind.

"Don't be afraid. I am the Lord God Almighty. You are not going to die. I have chosen you to spread my word," he said. His voice was a voice that stands all by itself. It cannot be compared to any other. It is distinguished by a burning fire that penetrates the mind and soul. The supernatural experience was unlike anything that happened in my whole life.

Those few words from Him would mark a turning point in my life and bring about a dramatic change in me. When the doctor came back in and checked me out, everything was normal. I had no more pain. God had healed me and spared my life. Finally, the doctor determined that I was as healthy as a horse. Later that night, I couldn't wait to tell my family the news-God had spoken to me. My family believed me and was happy. My dad was especially happy because now I would be carrying the word, just like him.

I had one brother who was skeptical. He had his doubts about God visiting me. The next morning, Mom and I stood at his bedroom door. I had no shirt on. When my brother awakened, he asked my mother why I had a cross on my chest. Mother explained that I didn't. I was bare-chested. God had to show him through a way he could understand that I had been called. God had to put a new mark upon me to dispel my brother's doubt. After hearing my mother explain it to my brother, I can't describe the joy I felt. For the first time, the mark symbolized something good. I knew that God loved me and I could finally be set free from the Mark of Cain.

During this time, Bo came by my house to see me. He was happy about his new membership to a well-known exclusive club. He said he was allowed to have guests, and he wanted me to go with him some night. I explained to Bo what had happened to me and that I was now on a new mission. Bo was so excited about this club, I don't think he heard anything I said. I wasn't too enthusiastic about going, but Bo was my friend and I decided to go. I made him agree that this would be a one-time thing. Bo was still wild and, anything went. I still loved him like a brother, but we were on two different roads in life.

When Bo and I arrived at the club, it was very extravagant. Bo was dressed nicely and so was I. We walked up to the door, and Bo showed the doorman his pass card to get in. The doorman said come on in, and Bo and I started to walk in. The doorman let Bo pass, but stopped me.

"Where do you think you're going?" he asked me.

"He's my guest," Bo told him

"No, sir," the doorman said. "He and his kind are not allowed." Bo and the doorman began to argue. This brought back memories of the restaurant. The doorman threatened to call the cops, and Bo was so furious, he took his membership card and tore it up in the doorman's face.

We went to another white club instead. It was a lot less extravagant, but at least we got in. It wasn't long, though, before trouble started again. While Bo and I were shooting pool, one white guy, who had obviously been drinking, began to shout about "the darkie" in the club.

"We don't allow no niggers in here" was all I could hear him shouting. He started to get some of the other white guys to join in the chant. Bo was concentrating so much on the pool game that I don't think he was aware of what was going on. Therefore, in the middle of the game, I suggested that we go. He wanted to know why, since the game was just beginning to get interesting. Bo complained, but we soon left without any violence. While Bo and I were riding together, I invited him to a black club that wasn't far away.

"We can finish our game of pool there," I said. Bo was all for it, so we went. When we went into the black club, we didn't have a problem. They accepted him. I heard no name-calling, and everybody was just doing their own thing. Bo and I played many games of pool and had a great time. I couldn't understand how my people could accept him but his couldn't accept me. After hearing the voice of God, I didn't dwell on the Mark of Cain much more. I suppressed it. I didn't want to think about it. I believed that even if it were true, I would rather be accepted secondary to God than not be accepted at all.

The following year, I went back to college. I didn't go back to Mississippi though. I went to a small black college in Alabama instead. I knew that if I was going to spread God's word, I needed to be well prepared. After finishing one year of school in Alabama, I went back home and completed my

Bible studies. By this time, I had learned a lot about God, but more importantly, I had built a personal relationship with Him. I would commune with Him every day. My faith in Him increased, and the Mark of Cain was forgotten once again. After being ordained by the Baptist church, I would often be called to speak at various churches around town. Before long, I was unanimously voted in as senior pastor of a Baptist church in the community. I became one of the youngest pastors in the area. What a challenge this was to my family and me. We all were elated. Truly, this was one of the happiest times of my life.

When I first took over the church, the membership was small. I had about twenty to thirty members. I had always believed that God's house should consist of different races. This was also my vision for my church. Through my job, I had gained respect from many whites and their associates and friends. I would invite them all to visit my small church. One Sunday morning while service was starting, I vividly remember looking over the small congregation of blacks and praying to God to honor my vision of unity. With my head down and the choir singing, I suddenly heard this loud shuffling of feet. When I looked up, I saw all the whites from my job, their families, friends, and associates. They also brought along Asian and Hispanic people. My heart was so filled with joy that my eyes filled with tears. I just stood and watched my vision unfold right before my eyes. The people seemed like they would never stop coming in. We had so many people that we had to get more chairs. We hardly had standing room. The black members looked on, and I could tell that most of them felt the same as I.

One minister leaned toward me and said, "This is great. With this integration of blacks and whites, you might have to transfer to a Southern Baptist church instead of Missionary Baptist." Neither he nor I had ever seen anything like this.

What a great day this was. Blacks and whites, Asians and Hispanics, all were praising the Lord together. At the end of the service, I extended the invitation to come to the Lord. All the guests came down to the altar and gave their hearts to the Lord. They also joined the church. I remember one elderly lady who couldn't stop dancing. She just kept praising God. She was the mother of a good friend I worked with and she had a tremendous influence on all the others. When she finally settled down from dancing, she shared her testimonial with me with tears in her eyes.

"I wanted to get back to the church," she told me. "When I came down to this altar, I felt a burden lifted. I love Jesus, and I am so happy to be here!" She hugged me around the neck and as the musicians started playing, we all danced and shouted together. I knew God was in our midst, because we all were in accord. What a blessed day this was. I knew this was the way God wanted it to be-all races, creeds, and colors worshiping together in spirit and truth.

For several Sundays, we continued to experience this joy and sweet communion at church. One night, the daughter of the elderly woman called me on the phone. She told me her mother had suffered a heart attack and was in the hospital. Immediately, I gathered some of the faithful members together to go pray for her. When we arrived at the hospital, she was in good spirits. This woman had a glow of beauty about her that you couldn't help but love. She was so happy to see us, and it made her feel good to know that we cared. We all joined hands, and I prayed for her. After the prayer, she thanked us and seemed content that God had heard our petition for her.

A few days passed, and I received a call from my friend, the elderly woman's daughter. She said her mother had been released from the hospital and she wanted to speak with me. I thought to myself that God had really moved quickly in this case. It had been only two days and she was already out of the hospital after a heart attack. When the elderly woman answered the phone, she was crying her heart out.

"What's wrong?" I asked her.

"I still have a heavy feeling on my chest," she told me. "I know I am not well." I suggested that she go back to the hospital, but she had tried that. "I tried to go back, I tried other hospitals, too. They said they had done all they could do, and I was okay." I found out the real reason that she couldn't go back to the hospital was that she had no insurance. I could feel the pain she was in.

"The Lord will ease your pain," I told her. I began to pray for her over the phone. A great calm came over her spirit after the prayer. She thanked me for praying for her and told me she was going back to bed. After hanging up the phone, I could hardly sleep, thinking about that lovely old lady. I was awakened by the telephone shortly after I went to bed. It must have been about two or three o'clock in the morning. When I answered the phone, it was my friend again. She was crying hysterically.

"Isaiah, my mother is dead," she managed to say. I was shocked and speechless. The pain of my friend and the loss of her mother pierced my heart. I just didn't expect it. Being that I was her pastor, I was asked to perform the eulogy. This would be the first funeral I performed as pastor. As I stood at the pulpit and gazed on the mourning family, I almost started to weep myself. I could feel their sorrow and loss, but I knew I had to hold up for the family's sake. I felt several emotions: sorrow, despair, and anger. I felt anger because the hospital would not admit her back in because of insurance purposes. This event would not have happened if a little more compassion were accepted, instead of money.

I kept my composure and delivered the message. I tried to comfort the family as much as I could, but could do very little because she was greatly loved and would be greatly missed. This was a healing only God and time could accomplish.

Many weeks passed after the funeral, but I kept in contact with the family. They had not returned to church, and I thought it was due to the death of their mother. I felt it was time for them to get back in church. It would help the healing process. I went to my white friend and questioned her about getting her family and friends back to church. Her response was slow and reluctant. It had nothing to do with the death of their mother. Her demeanor gave the appearance that there was something wrong with the church. She never did say exactly what. Later, I questioned a few of the faithful members about the status of our white members. I found out that some of the black members had made them feel unwanted. The gossip and the criticism about how they dressed couldn't help but be overheard by the whites. These few blacks felt that the whites should worship in their own church.

After I heard this, I was outraged. This was the very thing I stood against with all my being. All of a sudden it hit me. It was a reversal of the Mark of Cain. I had to see my friend soon and let her know that we loved her and her family and friends. I had to convince her not to listen to the ignorant few that hadn't grown in the Lord enough to know any better. When I expressed this to her, she told me the troubles were not new.

"Isaiah, you know we all love you. I didn't want to hurt your feelings by telling you how we were being ridiculed by some of the members in church," she said. "We kept coming because of you. You are sincere in what you're doing, and we wanted to be a part of it. However, I finally realized that continuing to worship with you would not enhance our spiritual growth. Instead of concentrating on God's word, we found ourselves focusing on what was being said about us. Knowing that we were not completely welcome in God's house made it very hard to be a part of your church." I was devastated by what she told me.

I tried with everything I had to get her and her family to come back. She rejected every offer. She was sure that it wouldn't work. Then I remembered the unbearable pain I felt from the Mark of Cain syndrome, the same pain she and her family were feeling, the same pain inflicted upon them by my people, the so-called black Christians. Deep down, I couldn't blame them for not coming back. I knew first-hand what it felt like to be an outcast and to not be accepted. This was the reversal of the Mark of Cain. It hurt me very badly that my people would do such a thing. After my friend made it evident they would not be back, I walked away sadly, but I promised myself that I would not give up on my dream. From then on, every message I preached would center on loving one another. I would do it until everyone saw the light. I was deeply sorrowed at heart.

I didn't give up on my white friends. Each day I went to work, I tried to encourage them to come back to church.

Each time, they refused. They seemed to drift further and further away from me. This just added more fuel to the message of loving one another I would bring every Sunday. I started to feel like I was not making any progress as pastor. I felt trapped. I wanted to bring God's message to a variety of people in all walks of life. People needed to start with the basics of loving their fellow man and see the big picture of what Christ is about before going any further into the doctrine of Christianity. People needed to know this was the reason Christ was sent, to show us the perfect example of love. To me, most church members were holding on to traditions of how their forefathers did things. They didn't want to change. They didn't want to see the truth that change must come from within, and God's laws of love must come alive in their hearts, for all mankind.

I started to bring in visiting ministers, white and black, of different denominations. These ministers would speak for me on appointed Sundays in hope that the people would become familiar with variety. This also gave me the opportunity to visit other churches. Most churches I visited were predominately white and of various denominations. I could feel the tension and uneasiness the members had with my presence. They tried to put on a good show of love and hospitality, but the façade can easily be discovered through the eyes. I had given the pastors copies of my ordination license, hoping that they would give me a chance to speak to their congregations, but I was never even recognized - even though I was just as much a pastor as they were. I was not invited to their pulpits. All I wanted was to bring the message of loving one another and to show how important it is for us to live together.

One Sunday, while visiting a predominately white church, I asked a head official, a deacon, about speaking to the congregation. He avoided answering me for a while and finally gave me an explanation.

"The congregation is just not ready for a black minister," he said. The answer threw me into a tailspin. Deep down, I think I had known it, but I had to hear it in order to believe it. All kinds of questions began to pop into my mind again. If the high officials, pastors, and ministers were not willing to do right and stand for unity, how was I to make a difference? How would I compete with the sophisticated degrees and eloquently spoken words of the preachers who were held in such a glorious light? I felt my little voice was not going to be heard and there was no possible way I could make a difference. In this moment of despair, my old nightmare rose up to haunt and torment me again. It was the Mark of Cain. In that moment, I felt like an outcast and a useless wanderer again.

For the next two weeks, I prayed to God. I wanted to resign as pastor. I felt I was inadequate. I was not producing, and no one was hearing my message. I was just spinning my wheels. During those two weeks, my next-door neighbor, a good friend of mine, asked me to counsel his nephew. When I spoke to his nephew, I learned he had been in prison. He said he had come to know the Lord, and he gave a tremendous testimonial that brought tears to my eyes. During my ministry, I had become friends with the chaplain at the country jail. I would often assist him in the chapel services. I thought it would be a good idea for the prisoners to hear this young man's testimony. When I contacted the chaplain the timing seemed to be just right. The chaplain was going out of town, and he wanted me to conduct the whole service for him.

That Sunday at the prison chapel, this young man knew

all the prisoners. They were glad to see him, and he was glad to see them. He sat in the audience with the prisoners while I conducted most of the service. Then the time came for the young man to speak. I called him up front. He came and gave a beautiful testimonial that left the prisoners standing, clapping, and in tears. Many of the prisoners came and confessed the Lord. I knew his testimonial would get this response. I was elated. I rejoiced all night about what took place in the prison chapel. I was still undecided about maintaining my pastor's position.

The next day, I received a call from the chaplain. I thought to myself, He *must have received the good news of that explosive service,* but it was totally the opposite. The chaplain informed me that the sheriff's detectives were planning to bring me in for questioning for drug smuggling. The young man I had brought in to give his testimonial had given more than that. He had brought drugs in for all his buddies. He had also told them that he would be assisting me and that each time he came to the jail he would have the stuff for them. An undercover detective had discovered all this. I was shocked beyond words.

"I am sorry, chaplain. I just didn't know," was all I could say.

"I know, Isaiah," he reassured me. "I knew you wouldn't have anything to do with something like this. That is why I explained and convinced the sheriff that you were innocent of any wrongdoing. That young man, however, is probably being picked up as we speak." He ended our conversation by telling me it would be best if I not assist him in the chapel for a while. As I sat quietly in my chair, That led me to believe that the sheriff was not so sure of my innocence. I started to examine my life, and the more I did, the mark of Cain became illuminated. Even though I tried to do well and was completely innocent, I was again seen as a fugitive.

This catastrophe was the deciding factor in my church endeavors. After three years, I resigned as pastor. Many cried and were deeply hurt. I resigned without giving any reason or explanation. I stepped down from the pulpit and didn't look back. I felt that I would try to live the way I believed instead of preaching it. I decided that if someone could view my life and could see the love of Jesus in me, God would be pleased. When I left the pulpit, I also changed my occupation. I went into security. My unwanted friend, the Mark of Cain, followed.

ᴛHREE

THE MEANINGLESS "MARK"

Before going into security, I had to take a security course. In the class, the Mark of Cain reared its ugly head. I was the only black man in the class, but that was no problem because I loved people. I actually had fun in the class until we came to the part of watching films. The film showed examples of those shoppers with the greatest potential to commit theft and crime. About ninety-five percent of these people were black. This explained why I was often watched as a fugitive whenever I went into a store. While I watched the films, all I could see was a fugitive and a vagabond. On a class break, the instructor apologized to me for the negative depictions in the film. He said it just wasn't fair that, because of your color, you are singled out as a criminal. As a retired cop, he had seen it happen many times.

"I must teach what the states requires," he told me.

I finished the security course with high marks and received my license. The first security job I was sent on was about fifty miles from my house. It was at a large power plant in the wilderness. The one thing that made my job enjoyable and interesting was the wildlife. It was amazing. The wild cats, deer, and, my favorite, the fox, would come close to me and not be afraid. Unlike humans who judged my outer appearance, I believed the animals sensed my spirit. Truck drivers for the plant saw this and were amazed.

One evening on my way to work, I met a pickup truck on the opposite side of the road. When the truck got closer, guys yelled something to me, but I couldn't make out what they said. I kept going and so did they. When I looked in my rearview mirror, the truck was turning around. It came up behind me very quickly, and I began to wonder what was going on. They began to ride my bumper. Looking in my rearview mirror, I saw it was a group of white men. They continued until they forced me off the road.

"You are on the wrong side of the tracks, boy," one of them yelled as they drove by me slowly and tauntingly. This scared me, but I went on to work. I knew this could be a dangerous situation. I was in the middle of nowhere, these guys could have killed me, and no one would ever know what happened. After work, I went into the office and brought this incident to my supervisor's attention. He brushed it off, saying they were just kids joking around and that it was nothing to worry about right now.

The next morning I was logging a truck out at the plant. When the truck pulled off, I went to back into the guardhouse. I heard yelling from the highway. When I looked, it was the same guys that ran me off the road. They pulled up in front of the plant.

"You are on the wrong side of the tracks, nigger!" they

hollered from the road.

There was also another pickup truck that followed them. They yelled out even more racist and hateful things and threatened my life. I was hurt, angry, and afraid. Even though these guys looked at me as if I was wearing the Mark of Cain, I was tired of running. I had to live, and that meant I had to work. I was determined not to let them run me from a job I loved. I didn't say a word back to them. I just went in the guardhouse and prayed for strength. When I brought this incident to my supervisor's attention, it raised his concern. He said he would notify the authorities in the area to be on the lookout for these guys. He also sent a new man to work with me.

"You should feel more comfortable," he said, as I left his office.

That evening, a new man did show up. He was a white man who looked like a real brawler. There were still no police in the area. As the night grew on, we became more acquainted with each other. He decided to go out on patrol while I stayed at command in the guardhouse. About fifteen minutes later, he burst into the guardhouse. He was as white as a sheet, his hair all frizzed out, and a look of sheer terror on his face. He quickly locked the door and called the cops.

"What happened?" I asked him.

"While I was patrolling, a bunch of guys in pickups and dirt-bikes chased me. They were firing guns and yelling 'nigger lover' and 'we gonna get you nigger lover' the whole time." He told the cops the same thing on the phone. After he hung up the phone with the cops, he immediately cut the lights off in the guardhouse. He was so scared, he hid under the table, shaking like a leaf. He kept saying, "I am not coming back, and if you know what's good for you, you won't either."

Minutes and hours passed, and there was still no sign of the cops. This caused my partner to become more frightened, almost hysterical. Sure, I was afraid, too, but I meant it when I decided I was not running anymore. I didn't make my black face, and I was not making any excuses. I would die standing my ground and for my integrity.

Suddenly a car pulled into the entrance of the plant. My partner was peeping out the window, praying it was the cops. It wasn't the cops, although it was a white man, banging on the door, yelling for help. I opened the door, and this man had the same frightened appearance as my partner's. The man began to tell the same story as my partner had told. He had stayed in the area, and two years ago, these guys burned his house down. He said he overheard these guys saying what they were going to do to this black guy (meaning me) and my partner. They had called him a nigger lover, too.

"I told them that was wrong, and they threatened my life. I came to warn you. These guys are serious. They have guns and a rope for him," he told us, pointing at me.

After this guy left, my partner crawled back under the table, trembling and wondering where the cops were. I knew the cops weren't coming. However, as daylight started to break, we realized we had survived the storm.

My partner crawled from under the desk.

"You can bet your britches you won't see me here again, and you better not come back. These rednecks will kill you," he said.

I didn't respond.

Sure enough, the next evening, he did not come back. I didn't want to, but deep down I knew I had to, but for some reason, each time I went back, I became less afraid and more confident. A few days went by without any trouble. One day after logging in a truck, I looked up, and there they sat, two truckloads of my enemies. They yelled insults and said how much they hated me and what they were going to do to me. I just stood tall, stuck out my chest, and stared them in the face, not saying a word, but thinking: *My Father made this black face, thick lips, and curly hair. Say what you will, but I am going to stand proud because I am a child of the King.*

After they yelled themselves hoarse, I turned and walked into the guardhouse. That was the last day I saw them. I continued to come to work, and there were no more problems. I knew I had scored a major victory by not running but instead standing and winning with non-violence. The meaningless words they used did not affect me or my integrity. I stayed at that job until I was promoted. The Mark of Cain followed.

I was promoted to an establishment of hi-tech security. This place dealt with a high volume of money. It consisted of many security officers. After about a month, I knew all the phases of my job. I had advanced to number-one rover. One night, all the other officers on my shift were waiting for me to come in. When I reported to work, they all were telling me about this new guy and how good-looking he was. When this guy came around, they all burst out laughing and when I saw him, I tried to refrain from laughing. I must admit it was hard.

This guy's hair stood straight up on his head. He was very pale. His shirt was three sizes too small. He wore high-water pants that were midway between his knees and ankles. He had a hearing problem, and when he spoke, it was real loud. My fellow comrades in security continued to make fun of him. They were not teaching him his security duties. They wanted him to fail. Everything that was said about him was negative. I took him under my wing and started teaching him the security procedures he needed to know. Eventually, he began to trust me and only me. My comrades saw my interest in him, and they honestly tried to help him. They were too late. He didn't trust them.

One evening while on patrol of the premises, Ned began to tell me about his life. He said he had three heart attacks and almost died. He said he didn't believe in God and he didn't like blacks because all through school they constantly picked at him. He said, he only had one true friend and that was his dog. His dog was everything to him.

As time went by, Ned became more comfortable with his job and me. He learned the security procedures and became a good officer. One evening when I reported to work, I saw all the security staff except Ned. When I asked where he was, they told me, with laughter, he's out back with his head down, all sad because his dog died.

"You would think he'd lost his best friend," someone said.

"He has," I told them. "You shouldn't joke about it." I went and found Ned and drove him around in the security truck for the entire shift. He cried nonstop and explained that his dog had been killed by a car. He was going to miss his best friend. Near the end of the shift, Ned said something to me that I never would have imagined.

"Now that my dog is gone," he began, "you are the only friend I have." This baffled me, because Ned was an older man who never liked blacks, and now he was calling me his only friend. I wondered how could I take on the responsibility of this lost and lonely man. As time passed, Ned recovered from the loss of his dog and became closer to me. I believed he saw something in the pattern of my life that drove him to love me, no matter what color I was. An incident at work proved this to me and sealed our friendship.

There was a jailhouse near where Ned and I worked. A new law was put into effect that allowed the less offensive and good prisoners to be released early. One night at work, I saw a young white kid, about sixteen years old, wander into our establishment.

My supervisor and other officers kept him in the lobby. I was going on break, but I overheard the kid pleading with them for help. He said he had been in jail for doing drugs and had been released early. He was feeling a drug craving coming on, and he wanted to stay clean. He was asking security to call one of the drug prevention programs to help him through his relapse. He was also very hungry. When I returned from my break, security still had the kid there. I had a few leftover chicken wings and fries in my hand that I was still eating. I thought the kid was staring at me, but he wasn't. He wanted my leftover food. I felt sorry for him so I reached into my pocket and gave him three dollars and some change-it was all I had. I told him to go in the cafeteria and buy something to eat. I quietly proceeded to my post in the parking area.

While I was on patrol in the security truck, my supervisor called me. He asked if I had seen the young man they were holding. He said one of the officers had seen me slip him something. Now, what I did for that young man came from my heart. I didn't want the whole world to know about it, but I had to explain, and everyone would hear because they all had radios. I told my supervisor that the young man was probably in the cafeteria eating. He was hungry, and yes, the officer saw me slip him a few bucks to buy food. My supervisor responded positively, and I was relieved.

I could tell by his voice that he knew he had neglected to do the good Christian thing for this kid. My supervisor was a devout Christian who went to church every Sunday and knew the Good Book well. He had far better means to feed this kid than I, but he hadn't seen the need. Later, I parked the truck and went into the cafeteria. I saw the young man eating and enjoying his food. He saw me and with his mouth still full of food, he thanked me.

I had a feeling that I had never had before. I also heard a spiritual voice identical to the one I had heard in the hospital.

"When I was hungry, you fed me."

Chills went all over my body. I felt God's presence and knew He was pleased with my good deed. After Ned heard this, his trust and friendship for me intensified.

Three months later, Ned had a massive heart attack. Ned's doctor called me at home. He said Ned had to have immediate heart surgery or he would die and that Ned had listed me as his only relative. The hospital needed my consent before they could operate, so I immediately gave it. I was startled by Ned's sudden illness, but more so by his using me as a relative. Ned hated blacks all his life. He would accept an animal before a black man, but now he was calling me brother.

The next morning, I called to the hospital to check on Ned. I knew the nurses would only give information to a relative, so when she asked who was I, I told her I was his brother. The nurse didn't believe me. She could tell my voice was the voice of a black man and to keep from getting into trouble, she transferred me to the doctor. The doctor was familiar with the relative situation and explained to me that Ned's operation had been a success.

Later that day, I went to the hospital to see Ned. When Ned saw me coming down the hallway, he acted like a little kid who hadn't seen his dad for months. While the nurses were working on him, he was saying, "Here he comes, here he comes, my brother." The nurses joked with him and said we did look alike. Ned was so happy to see me.

"I keep thanking God for bringing you through this serious operation," I told him.

"It wasn't God, it was you," he said, with a smile.

For a moment, I was stunned by his response because I thought he didn't believe in God. Ned went on to explain that he watched me live and trust an unseen God in all circumstances. Following my example, he turned his attention toward God to see Him for himself. This was a remarkable blessing I never saw coming. This once prejudiced, nonbeliever had found God through a black man. It was incredible. In the coming weeks, Ned regained his strength and health.

Meanwhile, I received a promotion on the job and became the night supervisor. I had worked my way up the ranks and earned this position. I loved it. The one man who was now my only supervisor impressed me as a good, honest, and fair man. Little did I know, he was a wolf in sheep's clothing. He would eventually be the one to cause the Mark of Cain to replay over and over in my mind. This man was the ideal charmer with an aura that shined like pure gold, but his heart was desperately wicked. He basically supervised the day shift but was also the manager of the night patrols. Each time the office would send him a new employee, if he was black, the manager would come to me with reverse psychology and almost taunt me.

"I have a new man here, and he's really good," he would say to me. "It's too bad you can't have him on your patrol." He was just hoping I would say I want him, and most times, I would. This went on until he had created a shift that was all black with the exception of a few white rejects that he didn't want. It was evident and confirmed by a reliable source that he wanted to keep his shift "lily-white" and apart from us.

I trained my team well. They had size, heart, and courage. Even though we worked at night, we emerged as the toughest and strongest security shift. This infuriated my superior. He started coming in early, before my shift had ended, just to antagonize and find fault with my men. Instead of having surveillance watching law-breakers, he had them watching my men and me. After returning to work from a day off, a young black man on my team came to me to make a complaint against the manager. He said the man criticized everything he did, cursed him out, and called him a nigger.

I immediately investigated and found the allegations to be true. When I confronted the manager about it, he quickly denied it. In fact, he said the young man cursed him out. When I confronted the witnesses again, they changed their stories. They did not want to challenge the authority of the manager. I was given little choice in the matter. The manager told me that I had better fire the employee or he would come back on me, and it wouldn't look good. I could see clearly what the manager was trying to do to this man, and I was not going to fall for it. Boldly, I stood up for my man and said I wouldn't fire him. His face turned cherry red, and he strutted off quickly in anger. He constantly found petty things that didn't amount to anything to pressure me into firing this man. Each time I said no, until one morning he finally used his own power.

"I tried to let you handle your people, but since you refused, I must do it," he said to me. Then he ordered me to fire the man and sign his papers. It saddened me to have to do it, but I had no choice. After this man was gone, the manager started in on another and then another until he demolished my whole crew, and I could do nothing about it. The Mark of Cain bore down heavily upon me because the manager did not want the black team to get any acclaim, so they had to go. We had become too good. We didn't stay in our place. Finally, I decided to die with my men by quitting the job that I had once loved so much. I never quit a job before having another one, but this was different. I would rather have died before giving up my integrity as a man and a leader.

Shortly after quitting this job, I ran into an old acquaintance who owned his own security business. He had wanted me to come to his firm years ago, but I had declined. When he saw me, he started telling me how good his company was doing. He said that he needed me, and I could go as high as vice-president, with money to match. I thought the timing couldn't have been any better. What a blessing! However, I was about to experience the other side to the Mark of Cain, and it's just as bad.

The owner was a church-going Christian and black,

like me. How could I refuse this offer? I started at the most prominent site in the company. He made me supervisor and filled my hands with responsibility that I welcomed. When he introduced me to my coworkers one thing struck me as strange-they were all black.

After my coworkers recognized I was in a position of authority and they felt comfortable with me, they began to reveal all the negative things about the company. Things like low wages, not being paid on time, and sometimes not being paid at all. There was an elderly man who had been with the company for a long time and backed up these complaints. I was astonished, and I told them that I would get to the heart of the matter. These people looked to me to make changes and positive progress for them.

When payday came, my salary was satisfactory, but my coworkers' salaries were not. The complaints from my coworkers began to come stronger and louder. When I spoke to the owner about my coworkers' money problems, he said he had been down this road with them for a long time and had always told them that he was not holding them here.

"If they don't like what is going on, they can leave," he told me. "Don't worry about these people. You're eating well, and your check is right, so what else do you want?" He promised that if I kept up the good work, it would get better and better for me. I didn't challenge this matter again for some time because I was well paid and eating the fat of the land. I turned a deaf ear to the cries and pains of my coworkers.

In a short time, the owner promoted me to vice-president and removed himself from the spotlight. He kept sole power behind the scene though. This caused the fire and the fury of the workers to come directly at me. One day, I hired a friend of a friend who happened to be white. This man was a good person and a strong worker. A significant change and turnaround came over me because of this man. I had no control over any of the finances. I would only distribute worker's paychecks to them. The key thing that I noticed was that the white man's pay was usually right, and if it wasn't, the owner quickly made it right. The blacks' paychecks were hardly ever right. The Mark of Cain syndrome rose up in me, and I no longer thought about me, but of those who were mistreated. I had to confront the owner about this matter again.

He basically said the same things as before, but this time he went even further. He said, if I didn't like what's going on, then leave. I could see the big picture. Even though he was just as black as us, he viewed us as having the Mark of Cain. Since my coworkers were black, he was using them for personal gain. He sacrificed honesty and integrity for his greed.

I had nothing to be proud of because I stood by and watched him do it. Soon he began to pour his fury and anger on me. My salary started coming sporadically, then cut in half. My livelihood was stricken, and I couldn't meet my bills. I was about to lose all that I had. I could now share the pressures of my coworkers because I was in the fire along with them. When I came to my senses, I relieved myself of this man and his company. My mother, father, sister, and brothers saw the licking of injustice I had taken from this man and came to my aid. They supplied the financial means and saved me from a great loss.

I quickly found a more substantial job in security and bounced back from my setback. It was on this job that I received the answers to the Mark of Cain question and brought it to a conclusion.

The job sent me on an assignment on the outskirts of town. Most of the people that lived out there were white and wealthy. My job was to greet them as they came in and to make sure their homes were protected. About fifteen percent of the people were sincerely friendly and went out of their way to welcome me, but the rest of the people made it known that they did not want me there. I believe this was why many of them moved to the outskirts of town, to escape the stereotypes like me.

Most times when I would greet them with "good morning" or "good evening" or "how are you doing?" they would give me a disdainful look and quickly turn their heads and speed on by the guard house. Many wouldn't even respect me enough to slow down or stop. They would totally ignore me. It made me feel useless and unwanted.

A cat lived on the premises. He was like a pet to all of the residents. The cat hung around the guardhouse a lot. The residents had supplied food in the guardhouse, and my added responsibility was to feed the cat. I took on that responsibility and made sure that the cat had food and water, because I am an animal lover, too. The only time most of these people would talk to me was to check on me to see if I fed the cat.

One day, I was asked to work a double shift, and when I reported to work I was tired and hungry. I had finished one shift and didn't have time to buy food. One of the residents, who had four small kids in the back, pulled up to the guardhouse. I politely came out and greeted her. She did not return the courtesy, but asked instead if I had fed the cat yet. While she was speaking, I was watching the kids in the back of the car. The kids were murmuring and saying things about me that only the parents have taught them. The woman heard them and tried to quiet them because they were embarrassing her. She quickly pulled away.

I was already tired and hungry, but this incident just added to my heavy and downtrodden heart. I went into the guardhouse and got the cat food and began to fill his bowl. When the cat began to eat, I thought to myself, *not one of these people asked me if I was hungry or if they could bring me some food.* The cat was loved and cherished more than a human. I loved the cat and was friendly to it, but the cat wouldn't let me come near it. At my lowest point, I guess I was looking for some appreciation or comfort from a cat. The blue-eyed, snow-white cat turned and looked at me, as though to say, "My belly is full, and that's all I need from you," and then trotted off. I knew even the cat rejected me. The people had taught him well. I slumped into my chair with grief, disgust, and hunger. The Mark of Cain overwhelmed me so much at this point that I begged for the Lord to speak to me.

Unlike other times, this was the first time He spoke to me concerning the Mark of Cain. His voice was not audible, but fire-piercing words penetrated my mind and demanded my undivided attention. He began to reveal His truths to me about the Mark of Cain.

"Isaiah, why do you continue to cry out to me about the Mark of Cain? I heard you years ago and answered you in my love letter to you, the Bible. Even though the answer was right there before your eyes, I knew you wouldn't grasp it from my word, so I had to let experience teach you, and now that it has, I come to you at this time. I heard you and knew your thoughts each time you agonized and felt despair about the color I made you. It grieved me, but the truth is, I love you. When I created man, I didn't say let us make a white man or a black man or any other color, I said, *"man."* You are a product of my great masterpiece, and I created you the color that I chose. Just as with all my other creations, different varieties and colors, but they are all special to me, even the smallest sparrow. Through this Klansman, you let Satan deceive you and caused you to bear needless worry and pain. I am familiar with the race problems and prejudices from all sides that go on in the world. So many people unfairly accuse me of being in agreement with all the injustices that go on. I have said my ways and thoughts are as far from yours as the heavens are above the earth. Let us examine some of my ways and thoughts concerning race and see what we come up with.

"In my love letter to you, do you remember what happened in the fourth chapter, John? Traditionally Jews had no dealings with Samaritans. Jews would go out of their way instead of going through Samaria. Jews felt they would be polluted if they touched the ground of Samaria, but I purposely went through Samaria because it was a thirsty woman there who needed that everlasting water, which only I could give. In doing this, I broke down all the race barriers and demonstrated that all are welcome at my table. You should have known that Satan was speaking through the Klansman. The Klansman preached hate, but I always preach love. In my word, what did I say to you concerning people like that Klansman?

"John's fourth chapter, first verse reads 'Beloved believe not every spirit, but try the spirits whether they are of God, because many false prophets are gone out into the world.' John, chapter four verses twenty and twenty-one say, 'If a man say I love God, and hateth his brother, he is a liar. For he that loveth not his brother whom he hath seen, how can he love God, whom he hath not seen.' The seventh and eighth verses of the same chapter say, 'Beloved, let us love one another, for love is of God, and everyone that loveth is born of God and knoweth God. He that loveth not knoweth not God, for God is love.'

"You showed a good illustration of love when you fed that hungry young man and had compassion for Ned. Even though they were of a different race, you cared. But each time I brought joy to your soul for these things, you would let the devil rob you, by dwelling on the Mark of Cain. Remember Hosea, fourth chapter, sixth verse: 'My people are destroyed for lack of knowledge. My hopes are that you and all believers grow more and more into my likeness.' John, chapter three, verse sixteen reads, 'For God so loved the world, that he gave his only begotten son, that whosoever believeth in him should not perish, but have everlasting life.'

"I enjoyed constant and unbroken fellowship in Heaven, but

I looked through the hourglass of time and saw you and all those who would be called by name. The world needed a savior, so down and down I did descend until I was made in the likeness of a man. Even though I had all riches of heaven and the cattle on a thousand hills were mine, I became poor that you might become rich. In heaven, I was never thirsty, but on earth, I thirsted that you might have everlasting water. I also never hungered, but on earth, I hungered in order to give you the bread of life. In heaven there is constant peace, joy, and happiness, but on earth, my heart was sorrowful, because the hearts of men were evil and desperately wicked. In heaven, I never was lonely, but on earth, I came to my own and my own received me not. This was done so that you might be comforted. In heaven's glory I was never tired or sleepy, but on earth, I was weary and slept so that you might rest in me.

"I came to bring the good news and tell men and women, boys and girls, that the Kingdom of God was at hand, but I was rejected and despised among them. Finally, they had a trial and condemned me to death. They took a whip to my back, tearing away my flesh with each lash. Even though I was God, I was also man, therefore, feeling the horrible pain from each lash. The hands that flung the whip to my back were hands that I fashioned. The mouths that yelled, 'crucify him,' mocked me, and spat upon me were the same mouths that I created. When they pressed that crown of thorns upon my head and pulled out my beard, they didn't realize it was because of me that they had health and strength to do all these cruelties to me. After they had heaped all their cruelties upon me, they pierced my hands and feet to a tree. They stretched me wide and hung me high.

"When they lifted me up, I had never felt so alone, because my father had imputed all the sins of the world upon me, sins such as murder, hate, lying, thievery, and adultery. I had no sin before, enabling me to be one with the Father, but now, even my Father turned his back. Through his pure and righteous eyes, he could not stand to look upon sin. This brought forth the cry from me, 'My God. My God. Why has thou forsaken me?'"

"But I loved man so much, I said, 'Father forgive them, for they know not what they do.' Finally, I cried. I hung my head on my shoulder and died so that men and women might live. Three days later I rose from the dead and now sat at the right hand of my Father, making intercessions for my people. When you were told you had to use a certain water fountain and restroom because of your color; when you were denied riding the pony; when you and your friends were hit with fruits because of your color; when you were not allowed in the same places because of your color; when you were feared and harmful and deadly weapons were pointed at you because of your color; when people thought more of pets than you because of your color ... I say unto you, all these things I have felt. I am acquainted with everything that is known to man. Furthermore, Isaiah, do you think what you went through as a black man can compare with what I went through to save the world?

"I say unto you now that the Mark of Cain is not the mark of a black person. Let that mark be between Cain and me. Stop dwelling on marks, signs, and symbols, and be filled with my spirit and it will guide you to all truth. When I live inside you, I will give you the strength to love those that hate you and spitefully use you. Be thankful for the color I made you, for each color is unique and special to me, but the heart of a man is the most important. The outside of a man means very little to me, but I ponder and search the heart. This is why I said to let the wheat and the tarot grow together and when I come I will do the separating, because I know my sheep and they know me.

"Parents are proud of their children. They love to see them grow and hear others say, 'He looks just like you,' or 'She has your eyes and nose.' I am also a proud parent, but who can say he or she has my eyes and nose, being that I am the spirit? Therefore, when my child gives a comforting word to the bereaved, he looks like me. When my child visits the sick and prays for their recovery, he looks like me. When you take time to visit the old and feeble and show them love, you look just like me. When my child tells men and women that the wages of sin is death, but the gift of God is Eternal Life, he looks just like me.

"If you are within my will, stop worrying about how people view you. People will pat you on the back today and tomorrow they are crucifying you. The bottom line is not how people view you but how I view you. People do not have a Heaven, or Hell, to put you in. Believe in me and do good and put the Mark of Cain behind you and strive for a new goal-that when you are in my presence when your life has ended, you will see me face to face and hear my voice say, 'Well done, my good and faithful servant. Welcome home.'"

Those were the last words the Lord's Spirit spoke to me about the Mark of Cain. His words gave me great joy and released me from a horrible plague. I couldn't help but think of all the blacks that feel like I did about the Mark of Cain. Many blacks have extreme despair about this. Feeling rejected and second class, they act out, and it results in murder, robbery, hate, drugs, and no regard for the gift of life. I feel compelled to try to get this message across, that God made and loves us all. Stop focusing on marks, colors, and races. There is a major issue going on in our country today concerning the Confederate flag. This brings to me a more personal side of my story concerning marks and symbols.

About eighteen years ago, I was married, and from this marriage, I received my most precious gift, my only son. My son was about seven years old when he and I were returning from church one Sunday. I stopped at a station to get gas. It was on a hill and at the foot of the hill was a major intersection. I pulled up to the gas pump and got out to pump, leaving my son inside the car. I went inside the station and asked the attendant for gas. He looked at me and asked for what car. When I looked back my car was rolling off down the hill and gaining speed. My young son was screaming for help. I took off with all the speed I had to rescue my son. Deep down I knew that I couldn't catch the car, because it had too much distance on me and it was headed right for the intersection with my son in it. My son was surely facing death. All of a sudden, out of nowhere, two guys ran across my path. One guy threw his body behind the car, slowing it up, while the other jumped in the car and applied the brake.

When I finally reached the car, I was so happy and grateful to those guys for saving my son. The guy that used his body behind the car had a broken leg. I offered my hand in gratitude, lifting him from the ground. When I asked what I could do for them, the injured guy hobbled to his feet, blessed me, and they both got in their truck and left. The moral to this story is about marks and symbols. Those two guys were white and wearing cowboy hats. Before they pulled off, I noticed a big Confederate flag on the back of the truck. In that one moment, that flag was beautiful to me. For, out of the goodness of their hearts, those guys risked their lives to save my son.

This is what Jesus wants us to do. He wants us to look beyond color and race and love one another. I hope and pray that those who are in turmoil and despair about the Mark of Cain will read this book and let it point you to the book of all books, the Bible. Let God enrich you with his love and free you from the bondage of the Mark of Cain.